T5-AXT-512

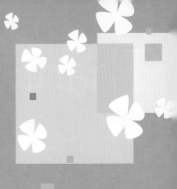

ARIEL BOOKS

Andrews McMeel
Publishing

Kansas City

Thanks

a Bunch!

Margaret Lannamann

Illustrated by Lisa Parett

Illustrations copyright © 2003 by Lisa Parett

ISBN: 0-7407-3374-5
Library of Congress Control Number: 2002111889

Thanks

a Bunch!

Introduction

Some people have an uncanny way of knowing when they are needed. They are always ready with a thoughtful gift, a lift to the auto mechanic, or brutally honest yet supportive words of advice. They offer help and friendship; they brighten our lives.

You are one of those extraordinary people. I hope the gift of this little book will express my appreciation for all you have done. You are the best—thanks a bunch!

Let us give *thanks:*

For generous *friends,* with

hearts—and smiles—as bright as . . .

blossoms.

—Max Coots

Thanks a Bunch!

Salute to Celebrities

*B*ronze star-shaped plaques have long been engraved and embedded in the sidewalk of Hollywood's Walk of Fame as a sign of appreciation for Hollywood's heroes: radio, TV, and stage performers, movie actors, directors, songwriters, and recording artists. Among the star-studded roster are two surprises: Lassie and Rin Tin Tin!

One can never pay in gratitude;

one can only pay *"in kind"*

somewhere else in life.

—Anne Morrow Lindbergh

Thanks a Bunch!

I *wish* I could always take

the time and just say, "Gee

whiz, thanks a lot."

—Chris Klein

Gestures of Gratitude

*O*nce, when I had done a favor for a friend, she thanked me by giving me a simple but lovely little music box. However, she told me that I was not to keep the music box; instead, I was to pass it on to someone whom I

Thanks a Bunch!

wanted to thank—which I did shortly thereafter. I sometimes wonder if that little music box is still being passed around the world somewhere.

—Mary, Sacramento, California

From the Heart

When Tom Brady won the Most Valuable Player award—and a fancy new car—after the New England Patriots' amazing victory in the 2002 Super Bowl, his astonished appreciation ("That's my car?") and sharing of his glory with his team ("We've got an MVT—Most Valuable Team") won the hearts of the many fans of this no-frills team.

W hen eating fruit, *think* of

the person who planted the tree.

—Vietnamese proverb

Thanks a Bunch!

True *generosity* grows in us as our *heart* opens.

—Jack Kornfield

You find true *joy* and *happiness* in life when you *give* and *give* and go on *giving* and never count the cost.

—Eileen Caddy

21

B_{eing} *thankful* is an

art to be cultivated and practiced

moment to moment.

—Oprah Winfrey

Thanks a Bunch!

World Recognition

The year 2000 was declared the International Year of Thanksgiving by the United Nations.

Feeling *grateful*
to those who have helped
us encourages us to do
kindnesses to others.

Gestures of Gratitude

I feel thanks for the driver who waves me ahead in traffic when he has the right-of-way but I'm in a bad spot; for my yoga instructor when she adjusts my posture beyond what I thought was my limit—and it feels terrific; for some-

Thanks a Bunch!

one who holds a door for me when she is carrying a big package and I'm not: for a friend who helps me see something in a new light.

**—Angela, Old Greenwich,
Connecticut**

Let us be *grateful* to people who make us happy; they are the charming gardeners who make our souls blossom.

—Jacques Prévert

Every relationship is one of give and take. *Giving* engenders receiving, and receiving engenders giving.

—Deepak Chopra

Golden Gratitude

*W*hen actor Ving Rhames was presented with the Golden Globe Award for best actor in a TV miniseries in 1998, he offered the award to Jack Lemmon (who was also nominated for the award), saying, "I feel that being an artist is about giving, and I'd like to give to you, Mr. Jack Lemmon." His extraordinary gesture elicited a standing ovation from the audience.

Saying *thank-you* auto-

matically reminds us of our place in

a greater scheme of things.

—Marianne Williamson

■

Thanks a Bunch!

Gratitude unlocks the

fullness of life.

—Melody Beattie

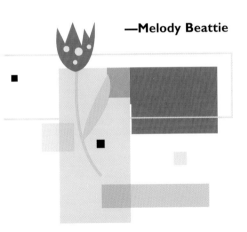

Say It with Stamps

*I*n October 2001, the U.S. Post Office unveiled a Thanksgiving stamp that pictured a cornucopia of fruit underneath the words "We Give Thanks."

Silent *gratitude* isn't

much use to anyone.

—Gladys Bronwyn Stern

Thanks a Bunch!

When you practice

gratefulness,

there is a sense of respect

toward others.

—Dalai Lama

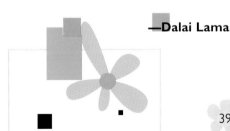

Gratitude: A warm sense of appreciation, of kindness received, involving a feeling of goodwill toward the benefactor and a desire to do something in return.

Life is an energy exchange of *giving and receiving.* The way to have what you want is to give what you need—emotionally and spiritually.

—Oprah Winfrey

The habit of *giving* only

enhances the desire to give.

—Walt Whitman

If you knew what I know about

the power of giving, you would not

let a single meal pass without

sharing it in some way.

—**Buddha**

Parade of Thanks

*T*icker-tape parades are a traditional way for New Yorkers to thank their heroes, whether they're athletes, aviators, war veterans, politicians, or explorers. This tradition dates back to 1886, when during a parade celebrating the dedication of the Statue of Liberty, office boys threw the curling streamers of ticker tape from windows along the parade route.

45

Anything that has real and lasting *value* is always a gift from within.

—**Franz Kafka**

Every day we need to tell some-one we *love* them. *Touch* them. *Thank* them for being.

—Elizabeth Taylor

It is well to *give* when asked,

but it is better to give unasked,

through understanding.

—Kahlil Gibran

Thanks a Bunch!

Gratitude lies at the heart

of the universe . . .

—Marianne Williamson

Gratitude makes sense of our past, brings peace for today, and creates a vision for tomorrow.

—Melody Beattie

G<small>reat</small> opportunities to *help* others seldom come, but small ones surround us every day.

—Sally Koch

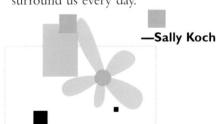

Thanks a Bunch!

Giving presents is a talent; to know what a person wants, to know when and how to get it, to give it *lovingly* and well.

—Pamela Glenconner

Happiness comes from giving, not getting. If we try hard to bring happiness to others, we cannot stop it from coming to us also.

—John Templeton

Kind words can be short and easy to speak, but their echoes are endless.

—Mother Teresa

Farsi   *mehr see*

Greek   *ef fah ree staw*

Japanese   *arigato*

Mandarin   *shyeh shyeh*

Thanks

a Bunch!

Around the World

Polish *jen koo yeh*

Taiwanese *do sha*

Turkish *sogal*

Urdu *shukria*

Gestures of Gratitude

When a friend of mine moved across town, I spent a weekend helping her pack up her stuff. She thanked me by treating me to an elaborate Chinese take-out dinner several days later. Imagine my sur-

Thanks a Bunch!

prise when, at the end of the meal, I opened a Chinese fortune cookie and found a beautiful handwritten note of thanks from her!

—Larry, Portland, Maine

To *give* without any reward, or

any notice, has a *special*

quality of its own.

—Anne Morrow Lindbergh

Thanks a Bunch!

We are *rich* only through

what we give, and poor only

through what we refuse.

—Anne Sophie Swetchine

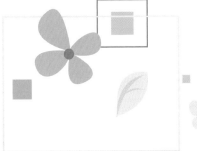

True gratitude, like true love, must find expression in acts, not words.

—R. Mildred Barker

Gratitude is not static. It is

an ever-flowing river.

—Anne Wilson Schaef

Not Just "Turkey Day"

Seven nations throughout the world—not counting the United States—have an official Thanksgiving Day: Argentina, Brazil, Canada, Japan, Korea, Liberia, and Switzerland.

Each day comes bearing its *gifts.* Untie the ribbons.

—Ann Ruth Schabacker

I can no other answer
make but *thanks* ...
and ever thanks.

—William Shakespeare

When I get too busy to stop and be *grateful,* I probably need to reexamine my priorities.

—**Anne Wilson Schaef**

That's what I consider true *generosity*. You *give* your all, and yet you always feel as if it costs you nothing.

—Simone de Beauvoir

69

When I look at my life through the lens of *gratitude,* all my experiences take on a rosy glow.

—Thomas Kinkade

Thanks a Bunch!

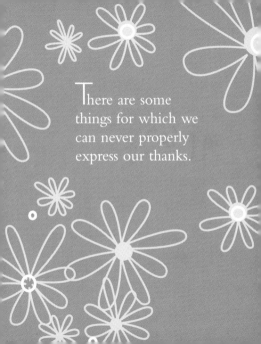

There are some things for which we can never properly express our thanks.

Global Gratitude

*T*he Center for World Thanksgiving at Thanks-Giving Square in Dallas, Texas, was established in 1981. The center, which is dedicated to revitalizing the spirit of thanksgiving, attracts visitors from all over the world. Favorite sites for tourists are the chapel with its unusual spiral tower, a peaceful courtyard, fountains, and gardens.

Gratitude opens your

heart to *inspiration.*

—Dr. John F. Demartini

Thanks a Bunch!

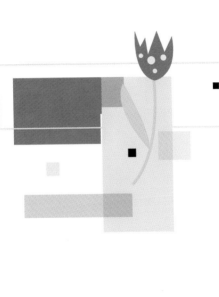

A 225-Ton Thank-You

*I*n 1886, the Statue of Liberty was given to the United States by France in appreciation of and admiration for the American ideal of human liberty. The statue has since become one of the best-known landmarks in the world, welcoming visitors to New York harbor and serving as a symbol of freedom.

For all that has been, *thanks.* For all that will be, *yes.*

—**Dag Hammarskjöld**

*Book design and composition
by Diane Hobbing
of Snap-Haus Graphics
in Dumont, NJ*

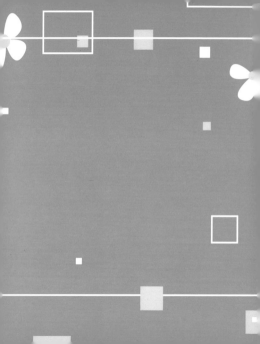